THE SCIENCE OF...
SEARCHING FOR
LIFE IN SPACE

by
CLINT TWIST
Consultant
OLIVIA JOHNSON

ticktock
MEDIA

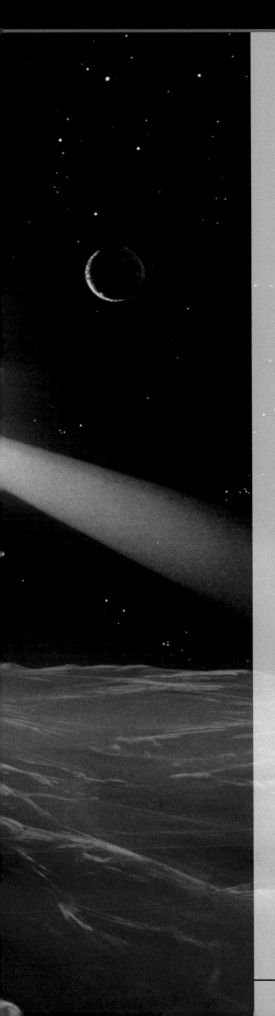

CONTENTS

People have been studying night skies and the **stars** for thousands of years. Ancient astronomers in different lands all gave different names to the brightest stars in the sky. They also gave names to the constellations – the patterns that some stars appear to form in the sky. The Greeks knew that most stars remain in the same fixed pattern, but that some appeared to travel across the sky. They gave the name '**planets**' to these wandering stars. For many years, people accepted the ancient Greek idea that the Earth was at the centre of the **universe**, and that the **Sun**, the stars, and the planets all revolved in **orbit** around the Earth.

THE EARTH IN SPACE

Following the invention of the telescope in the 16th century, astronomers were able to get a better view of the universe, and developed a better understanding of how it operated. They realized that the Earth and the other planets actually orbit around the Sun; and that stars are in fact distant suns — very distant indeed as it turns out. As the science of astronomy progressed, with bigger and more powerful telescopes, more and more discoveries were made. Astronomers were able to view distant galaxies, and work out the life-cycle of stars. They also discovered planets, such as Neptune and Pluto, that were unknown to ancient astronomers. During the 20th century, astronomy took a giant leap forwards with the introduction of radio telescopes, artificial satellites, and spacecraft. Scientists were able to study images of strange and fascinating objects, such as **supernovae** and **pulsars**.

This observatory at Mauna Kea in Hawaii is constantly observing the stars and planets of our solar system and beyond.

If there is life in space, it is highly unlikely it will look like this monster, taken from the film Alien.

EXTRATERRESTRIALS?

As scientists learnt more about the universe, they began to wonder about the possibilities of other forms of life — **extraterrestrial** life. During the 19th century, one astronomer announced that he had discovered artificial canals on the surface of Mars — a sure sign of extraterrestrial life. His discovery turned out to be mistaken, and some scientists predicted that we would never find life outside the Earth. So far, these predictions have proved to be true. When astronauts landed on the **Moon** in 1969, they found no signs of life; and robot spacecraft have since found no evidence of life on Venus, Mars, or any other of the planets. But, and in science this is a big but, just because we have found no evidence of yet, it does not mean that extraterrestrial life does not exist. It just means that we have not found it yet, and that is no reason to give up the search.

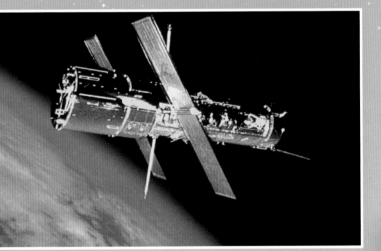

The Hubble Telescope has allowed astronomers to see far beyond our Solar System.

Astronomers have learnt to expect the unexpected when studying the universe, and they have discovered many strange and wonderful things. They have photographed the birth of new **stars**, and have detected the strange objects that are created when old stars explode. Some people are convinced that it is only a matter of time before astronomers catch sight of alien spaceships speeding towards Earth.

ALIEN INVASION

The idea of invaders from another **planet** is more than 100 years old. At the end of the 19th century the author H. G. Wells wrote a popular novel entitled *War of the Worlds*, in which Martians armed with futuristic war machines and death-rays invaded Earth. In 1930s, to celebrate the 40th anniversary of the novel, the actor Orson Welles produced a dramatised version for American radio. He made the story of the Martian invasion sound like a news report. When the dramatisation was broadcast, it sounded so realistic that thousands of people believed that Martians actually had invaded Earth.

SEARCHING THE SYSTEM

Today, scientists think it is very unlikely that aliens from another planet will invade us. They have examined all of the other planets in the **Solar System**

War of the Worlds created panic when it was first broadcast on radio among a public who did not realise it was fictional.

with telescopes and with spacecraft sent from Earth, and none of them show any signs of life. If scientists do eventually discover life elsewhere in the Solar System, it will probably be primitive **bacteria** rather than an advanced civilization capable of invading Earth. However, just because scientists think an alien invasion is unlikely, it does not mean that they think it is impossible. The more scientists learn about the universe, the more they realize how little they actually know for certain. Until about ten years ago, the idea of planets outside the Solar System was just a theory without any proof. And when the proof was finally found, it was completely unexpected.

SCIENCE CONCEPTS

THE SPEED OF LIGHT

The universe is so large that scientists measure it in light years. A light year is the distance that light travels in one year. Light travels at about 186,000 miles per second, and one light year is approximately equal to 5,875 billion miles. Light from the Sun takes about 8 minutes to travel the 93 million miles to Earth; and so Earth can be described as being 8 light-minutes from the Sun.

This stunning image was taken by the Hubble Telescope, and shows an array of distant galaxies, many light years from Earth.

LIMITED VIEW

Telescopes get bigger and better each year, but the universe is a very, very large place and it is full of strange things. Even the best telescopes can only provide astronomers with a few brief glimpses of what is really happening in the universe. Stars are the most numerous objects in the universe — there are billions and billions — but stars like the Sun are actually quite rare. Some stars are much younger than the Sun, and have only just been formed inside dust clouds. Some stars are much larger than the Sun, and are likely to blow apart in a gigantic **supernova** explosion that leaves behind a **neutron star**. Some stars inflate slowly and change colour, while other stars seem to shrink and fade away. Around some of these stars there may be planets that support life; the question is, "Which stars?"

This film still, taken from the 1955 movie This Island Earth, reflects a popular idea of the time as to what aliens might look like.

SCIENCE SNAPSHOT

Scientists use images taken by the Hubble telescope to create beautiful "false color" images of nebulae, galaxies, and other celestial bodies. After they delete the cosmic-ray streaks, they use four filters that see the light produced by specific atoms in the objects. The blue, green, and red filters screen for oxygen, hydrogen, and sulfur atoms, respectively. When combined with the fourth filter (a starlight filter) a breathtaking final image results.

The nearest star to Earth is the **Sun**, a bright yellow **star** that produces plenty of light and heat. Our star is fairly unusual, only about 5 percent of stars produce as much heat and light as the **Sun**. There are nine planets orbiting the Sun. Our star and its **planets** make up what is known as the **Solar System.**

OUR LOCATION

The Sun is located in one of the spiral arms of the **Milky Way Galaxy**. A galaxy consists of billions of stars held together by the force of **gravity**, and most galaxies also contain vast clouds of dust and gas. The Milky Way Galaxy is shaped like a huge lens — fatter in the middle than at the edges. The whole galaxy is rotating, and this rotation has produced several spiral arms that extend from the centre. The Milky Way Galaxy measures about 100,000 light years in diameter. The nearest similar galaxy is the Andromeda Galaxy about 2 million **light years** away.

The Sun with the planets Mercury (top) to Pluto (bottom).

SCIENCE CONCEPTS

GRAVITY RULES

Gravity is the force that shapes the objects in the universe and holds them in place. It is the strongest force in the universe and the only force that operates over long distances. Gravity is a property of matter – we experience it as an attracting force between objects. The more mass (matter) an object has, the stronger its gravity. The Earth's gravity is strong enough to hold you in place on the surface and prevent you from flying off into space. The Sun has millions of times more mass than the Earth. The Sun's gravity is strong enough to hold the planets in their orbits over distances of hundreds of millions of kilometres.

Compared to other stars, the Sun is actually quite close to Earth.

ORBITING AROUND A STAR

Held by gravity, the planets orbit around the Sun as if they were attached to it by pieces of invisible string of varying length. Earth is the third planet from the Sun. Mercury and Venus are closer, and the other planets are further away. Earth orbits the Sun at a distance of about 150 million km, and takes one year to complete one **orbit**. Jupiter orbits at a distance of about 780 million km, and one orbit lasts nearly 12 Earth years.

A RANGE OF PLANETS

The planets in the Solar System can be divided into two basic types, small rock planets and large gas planets. Mercury, Venus, Earth, and Mars are rock planets. Jupiter, Saturn, Uranus, and Neptune are gas planets. Pluto is too distant for scientists to be certain exactly what it is. Most of the planets have one or more moons (natural satellites) orbiting around them. Jupiter is by far the largest of the planets. With a diameter of about 143,000 km, it is one-tenth the size of the Sun. Jupiter contains more than twice as much mass as the other nine planets put together.

Our Sun is a burning ball of gas 300,000 times the size of Earth. By burning hydrogen it provides the energy that is essential to life on Earth.

SCIENCE SNAPSHOT

The planets in the Solar System can give the mistaken impression that space is a very crowded place, when in fact the opposite is true. Earth is only eight light minutes from the Sun, and the diameter of the whole Solar System is about 11 light hours. By comparison, the nearest star –-Alpha Centauri C – is about 4.25 light years away.

Water is essential to life on Earth. The surface of the planet is mainly covered by water.

Earth is a very comfortable place to live. More than one million different species of life have been identified on Earth, and scientists believe there are millions more that are still to be discovered. So far as we know, Earth is the only place in the **universe** where life exists. What is it that makes Earth so special?

WATER

Although there is plenty of dry land, two thirds of the Earth's surface is mainly covered by water,. Some of the water is frozen into ice, but most of it is liquid, as salt water in the seas and oceans. Some of this evaporates and falls on land as fresh water, so that plants can grow and animals may drink. But there is more to water than just drinking. The bodies of most living things (including humans) are composed mainly of water in liquid form. Water can only exist as a liquid when the temperature is between 0 C and 100 C, and most species can only survive within a much narrower range of temperatures. One of the main reasons there is life on Earth is because the planet receives just the right amount of energy from a **star** to produce mild surface temperatures.

Conditions on Earth are perfect for a variety of life to flourish.

SCIENCE CONCEPTS

A VITAL ELEMENT

The incredibly complicated chemistry that takes place inside every living thing is based on the chemical element carbon. Life on earth is often described as carbon-based life, and this is the only sort of life that we know and understand. Carbon-based life exists on Earth because conditions here allow it to exist. Most scientists believe that if we find life elsewhere in the universe, it will be carbon-based. In theory, however, life based on a different chemical element could exist under conditions very different from those on Earth.

Earth's gravity allows it to retain an atmosphere that can support a great variety of life.

AIR

Another essential thing about Earth is that there is plenty of oxygen to breathe. A mixture of oxygen and other gases, such as nitrogen and **carbon dioxide**, forms a thick **atmosphere** around Earth. We call this mixture of gases **air**. As well as allowing us to breathe, Earth's atmosphere helps keep temperatures mild, and allows water to circulate as rain. It also shields Earth from some of the Sun's harmful energy — most UV light for example. You cannot see the atmosphere, but you can see the clouds of water droplets that often float in the atmosphere above Earth's surface.

MAGNETISM

Although Earth is mainly composed of rock, the planet has an iron core. As the Earth rotates, the iron core produces a strong magnetic field around the planet that deflects most of the Sun's harmful energy away from the Earth. Without this magnetic field, Earth's atmosphere would be "blown" away into space by the energy streaming out of the Sun.

✎ SCIENCE SNAPSHOT

THE GOLDILOCKS ZONE

Earth orbits the Sun inside what scientists call the Goldilocks zone – the region around a star where conditions are suitable for carbon-based life. The Goldilocks zone of a star is fairly narrow. Venus and Mercury are too close to the Sun to be in the zone and they are too hot for life to exist. Mars is just inside the zone, but has other problems. The other planets are too far away to be in the zone, and are much too cold.

Mars is the nearest planet to Earth. It orbits the **Sun** at a distance of about 228 million kilometres, near the outer edge of the **Goldilocks zone**. People have long wondered about the possibility of life on Mars. Spacecraft from Earth that have landed on the planet have not yet found any evidence of life.

DRY AND COLD

Bare rock, stones and dust cover the surface of Mars — there is very little else. Near the north and south poles the ground has a light coating of frozen **carbon dioxide**, but that is all. The planet has a very thin **atmosphere** composed mostly of carbon dioxide gas. Mars is a hostile environment, during the Martian day the surface is bombarded by dangerous UV light, at night temperatures fall to −120°C. There is absolutely no water, either liquid or frozen, on the surface of Mars. It is a cold, dry, airless planet, swept by strong winds that create vast dust storms. Conditions on Mars are not now suitable for carbon-based life. Long ago, however, conditions there may have been different. It seems as if life may once have had a chance on Mars.

The Mars Polar Lander was launched on the 3rd January 1999 and landed on Mars on the 3rd December 1999.

SEARCHING FOR LIFE

Spacecraft have examined most of Mars' surface with powerful cameras, and robot landers have examined small portions of the surface in the tiniest detail. There are no signs of any plants or animals, even very small ones. The landers have also carried out chemical tests to see if there are any substances on Mars that may have been produced by microbes, such as **bacteria**. All these tests have proved negative — there is no sign of life on Mars. The landers have, however, found evidence that there was once water on Mars.

SCIENCE CONCEPTS

LOST ATMOSPHERE

Millions of years ago Mars had an atmosphere similar to Earth's. However, Mars was too small and too rocky to hold onto its atmosphere. Mars is only about half Earth's size; it has much less mass and its **gravity** is much weaker. Mars' gravity was not strong enough to prevent most of its atmosphere from gradually drifting away into space. The problem was made worse because Mars does not have an iron core, so there was no magnetic field to protect the planet's atmosphere from the damaging effects of the Sun's energy. Without strong gravity and magnetic protection, the Martian atmosphere was doubly doomed.

Mars

Earth

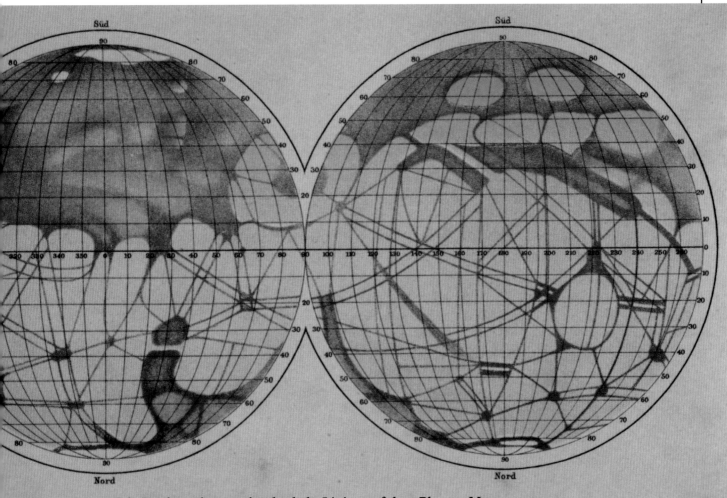

Die Verdoppelungen der dunkeln Linien auf dem Planten Mars,
nachgewiesen hauptsächlich während der Oppositionen von 1882 und 1888
von J.V.Schiaparelli.

A ONCE WATERY WORLD

The surface of Mars has some large features that look very like dried up rivers, but scientists could not be sure that they were formed by water. By examining Martian rocks very closely, landers have found evidence that some of these rocks were formed in the presence of water. This proves that there was once water on the surface of Mars — and where there was water, there may have been some form of life. Some scientists believe that a long time ago Mars had oceans, rivers and a thicker **atmosphere**. The planet was too small and rocky to hold onto these precious resources, and they were lost into space.

Historical map of the surface of Mars, by the Italian astronomer Giovanni Schiaparelli (1835-1910).

SCIENCE SNAPSHOT

Some of the meteorites that land on Earth are believed to come from Mars – they are bits of the planet's surface that have been kicked into space by other meteorite impacts. Some scientists claim to have found evidence of life in these Martian meteorites. Using high-powered microscopes they can see tiny blobs that look like the remains of living cells. Most scientists, however, are not convinced that these blobs are evidence of life.

An array of radio telescopes beneath a large, false-color image of the Whirlpool Galaxy.

Radio signals, like light, can travel to Earth from distant **stars** and **galaxies**. All the signals that have so far been detected have proved to be just radio "noise" produced by a variety of natural sources. But among all this noise, there just might be some radio signals produced by other forms of intelligent life. Radio astronomers use large metal dishes (known as radio telescopes) to detect these radio signals coming from space.

RADIO ASTRONOMY

Looking at the skies through radio telescopes has provided scientists with lots of important information. Radio telescopes "see" the same universe as ordinary telescopes, but they present a very different picture. Objects that produce very little light may appear very "bright" when viewed through a radio telescope. So far, all the radio signals from space that have been detected have come from natural sources. The most powerful signals are generated by the shockwaves and magnetic fields created by **supernovae** and **black holes**. The weakest radio signals are produced by vibrating gas molecules drifting through space.

SCIENCE CONCEPTS

VISIBLE SPECTRUM

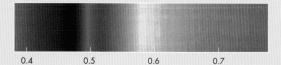

0.4   0.5   0.6   0.7

THE ELECTROMAGNETIC SPECTRUM

Radio signals, visible light, microwaves, and X-rays are all types of electromagnetic energy. This energy travels through space as waves. The different types of energy have different **wavelengths**, and these are arranged in what is known as the electromagnetic spectrum. The coloured spectrum of light is just a small part of electromagnetic spectrum. Radio signals have wavelengths from about 1 millimetre to one kilometer; the wavelength of visible light is measured in ten-millionths of a millimeter. X-rays and gamma rays have wavelengths that are up to a million times shorter than those of visible light. **Gravity** is not part of the electromagnetic spectrum, and scientists do not yet fully understand how it operates.

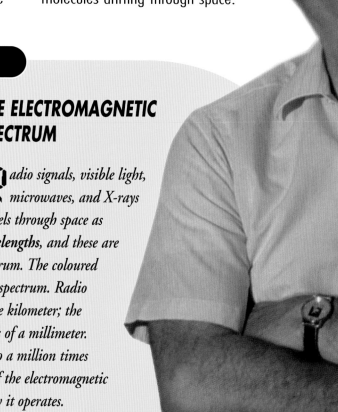

SETI

In the 1960s a group of scientists decided to use radio astronomy to search for signs of life elsewhere in the universe. This project became known as the Search for **Extraterrestrial** Intelligence (**SETI**). Before the search could begin, the scientists had to decide exactly what they were searching for, and where to look for it. The first stage was easy. They realized that intelligent beings would repeat a radio message over and over again; therefore they had to search for signals that repeated in an unnatural pattern. Deciding where to look was more difficult.

Frank Drake and Jill Tarter lead the SETI team, the Search for Extraterrestrial Intelligence. They stand beneath the radio telescope they will use to look for radio signals from space.

PULSARS

Scientists searching for radio signals as a sign of intelligent life must be careful that objects such as **pulsars** do not fool them. A pulsar is a powerful radio source that appears to "beep" regularly. The first pulsar to be discovered beeps every 1.3 seconds. Many more pulsars have been found, and some of them beep hundreds of times a second. A pulsar is a rapidly rotating **neutron star**. Because it is made from **superdense** matter, a neutron star has incredibly strong gravity and generates very powerful magnetism. As the star rotates, it sends out two beams of radio energy. Each beep is a "flash" of radio energy as one of these beams sweeps across the Earth.

SCIENCE SNAPSHOT

The SETI project continues to search the radio skies, and thousands of nearby stars have been examined, but so far without success. SETI scientists are concentrating their search in the microwave portion of the electromagnetic spectrum, because it contains the wavelength produced by vibrating **hydrogen** gas molecules. The scientists believe that other intelligent beings would choose this "hydrogen wavelength" for communication between the stars.

Planets are very small compared with **stars**, and **planets** orbiting around distant stars cannot be seen from Earth, even with the most powerful telescopes. However, astronomers have learnt how to use their telescopes to detect the presence of distant planets. The use special techniques to watch the planets make their stars wobble.

Professor Carlos Calle adjusts interferometry laser equipment in the Optics Laboratory.

GRAVITY WOBBLES

Stars wobble because **gravity** is a two-way force. A star's gravity is strong enough to hold planets in their **orbits**; but planets also have gravity, and this can have an affect on the star. Although we think of the **Sun** as being a stationary fixed point at the centre of the **Solar System**, our star actually follows a very small orbit through space. The planets of the Solar System shape the Sun's orbit. As the planets travel in their orbits, their gravity tugs at the Sun causing it to slightly shift its own orbit. When viewed from afar, these shifts in a star's orbit make it appear to wobble regularly. If you could look at the Sun from a distance of ten light years, you would be able to see the wobble caused by the gravity of the two largest planets, Jupiter and Saturn. Wobble watching is the best way of detecting planets around distant stars, and astronomers have two methods of measuring wobble.

INTERFEROMETRY

One advanced technique relies upon measuring a star's position very accurately every night for several months. Any wobble will cause the star's position to vary slightly. By comparing results over a long period of time, astronomers can tell whether the star is wobbling or not. Measuring the position of a star accurately with a single telescope is very difficult. The best results are obtained using **interferometry**, a technique that uses two different telescopes to simultaneously measure the position of a star. The two sets of measurements are then combined mathematically to give one very accurate position.

SCIENCE CONCEPTS

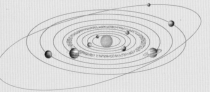

The orbit of each planet around the Sun represents a delicate balance between the powerful tug of the star's gravity and the forces produced by a planet's high-speed motion through space. The Earth, for example, orbits at a speed of about 60,000 mph. For the innermost eight planets, this balance of gravity and motion produces almost perfectly circular orbits that all lie within the same flat plane. However, the outermost planet, Pluto, has achieved a different balance. Its orbit is strongly elliptical and it is at an angle to the plane of the other planetary orbits.

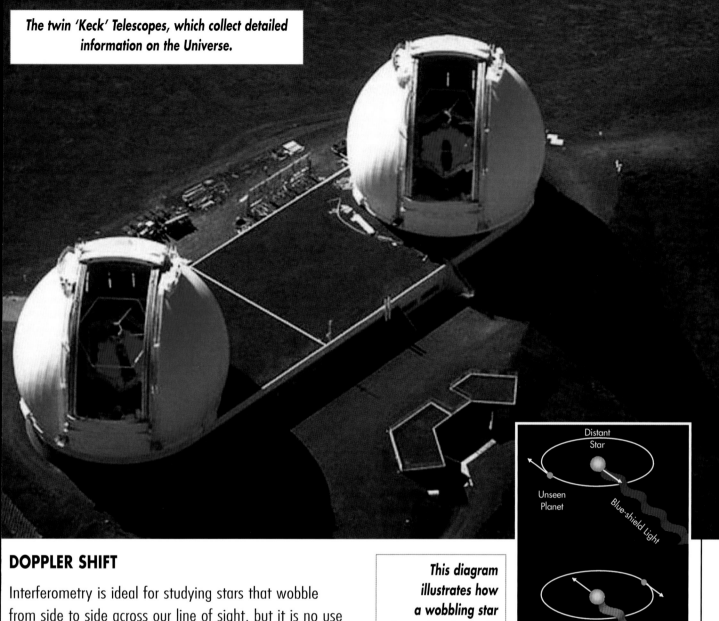

The twin 'Keck' Telescopes, which collect detailed information on the Universe.

Distant
Star

Unseen
Planet

Blue-shield Light

Red-shield Light

DOPPLER SHIFT

Interferometry is ideal for studying stars that wobble from side to side across our line of sight, but it is no use for detecting stars that wobble back and forth along our line of sight. Objects moving along our line of sight — either towards or away from us — can be studied using the **Doppler technique**. In order to tell whether a **star** is wobbling in this way, astronomers pay close attention to the colour of its light. If a star changes colour slightly on a regular basis, then it may well be wobbling. Light from an approaching object looks bluer than normal (this is called the blue shift), and light from an object moving away looks redder than normal (the red shift). If a star's light regularly shifts from red to blue, then the most likely explanation is that it has planets that are making it wobble.

This diagram illustrates how a wobbling star is used to detect the presence of a planet.

SCIENCE SNAPSHOT

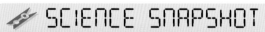

Astronomers made an incredible discovery when they began studying distant galaxies with the Doppler technique in the 1920s – the **universe** is expanding. The light from all distant galaxies is red-shifted, which shows that they are moving away from us. The only explanation for this red shift is that the universe is constantly expanding in all directions.

By the end of the 1980s there were several teams of astronomers searching the night sky for signs of **extra-solar planets** (planets outside the Solar System). They were convinced that these planets existed, but they had no proof. When they did find proof, it was not what they had expected.

PLANETS AROUND PULSARS

The astronomers who made the first discovery were not looking for planets around nearby stars. They were using radio telescopes to study the faint **pulsar** PSR B1257+12 more than 1,000 **light years** from Earth. The pattern of radio signals from the pulsar was not perfectly regular. The astronomers realized the only explanation for the irregularity was that the pulsar had planets. The **gravity** produced by the planets was making the pulsar wobble very slightly, causing the irregularity in the radio signals. After taking additional measurements, the astronomers were able to prove that three small planets **orbited** round PSR B1257+12. Each planet is about the same

This illustration is of a pulsar as seen from a nearby planet. Pulsars rotate so rapidly they appear to flash like a lighthouse.

size as Earth or Mars, and takes between 25 and 99 days to orbit the pulsar. They have not been named, and are known by the letters a, b, and c. Scientists do not believe that there is life on these pulsar planets. If they existed before the **supernova** that produced the pulsar, they will have been burned clean by the explosion. If they were formed during the **supernova**, life will not have had time to develop. Also, if the pulsar's radio beam sweeps across the planets, the radio energy at close distance would kill anything living.

SCIENCE CONCEPTS

FAMILIAR PATTERNS

We are now certain that the **Sun** is not the only star with planets, but we have not yet discovered any other systems of planets like our own Solar System. Most of the **extra-solar** planets so far discovered follow the same pattern as 51 Pegasi b – a single large planet orbiting very closely around a star. These planets are known as Pegasian planets, and they appear to be the most common type of planet in the **universe**.

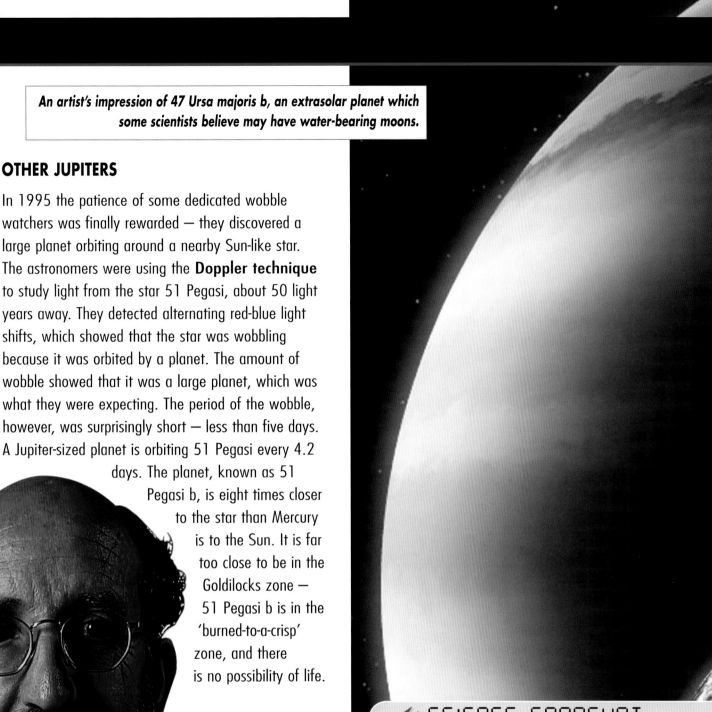

An artist's impression of 47 Ursa majoris b, an extrasolar planet which some scientists believe may have water-bearing moons.

OTHER JUPITERS

In 1995 the patience of some dedicated wobble watchers was finally rewarded — they discovered a large planet orbiting around a nearby Sun-like star. The astronomers were using the **Doppler technique** to study light from the star 51 Pegasi, about 50 light years away. They detected alternating red-blue light shifts, which showed that the star was wobbling because it was orbited by a planet. The amount of wobble showed that it was a large planet, which was what they were expecting. The period of the wobble, however, was surprisingly short — less than five days. A Jupiter-sized planet is orbiting 51 Pegasi every 4.2 days. The planet, known as 51 Pegasi b, is eight times closer to the star than Mercury is to the Sun. It is far too close to be in the Goldilocks zone — 51 Pegasi b is in the 'burned-to-a-crisp' zone, and there is no possibility of life.

The astrophysicist Michel Mayor discovered 51 Pegasi B in 1995.

A GREAT DISCOVERY

One star may have a whole system of planets. Astronomers have detected a Jupiter-sized planet orbiting around the star 47 Ursa majoris. This planet (called 47 Ursa majoris b) differs from Pegasian planets because it orbits the star at about the same distance as Mars is from the Sun. Although it has not yet been confirmed, 47 Ursa majoris may well have one or more Earth-sized planets orbiting within its Goldilocks zone.

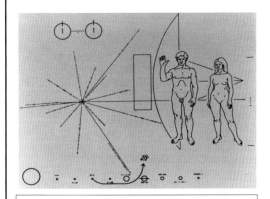

This plaque, attached to the Pioneer 10 & 11 spacecrafts, indicates their origin in case they are examined by another intelligent species.

Some scientists argue that there must be other forms of intelligent life somewhere among the billions and billions of **stars** in the **universe**. Logically, there is no reason why Earth should be unique. By the same logic, some of those other forms of life should be a lot more intelligent than us – advanced intelligences with very advanced technology.

FRUITLESS SEARCH?

Astronomers have been searching the sky for signs of intelligent life for nearly 50 years. So far they have found nothing whatsoever to suggest that there are other intelligences out there. One reason for this may be that advanced intelligences may use their advanced technology in ways that we can only imagine. In order to take maximum advantage of a star's **Goldilocks zone**, they might construct a vast hollow sphere around the star, hiding it from view. Another reason might be that the **universe** is a very dangerous place, full of hostility and war. An advanced intelligence might decide that the best thing to do was to conceal all traces of its existence. No wonder we cannot find them if they are hiding from us!

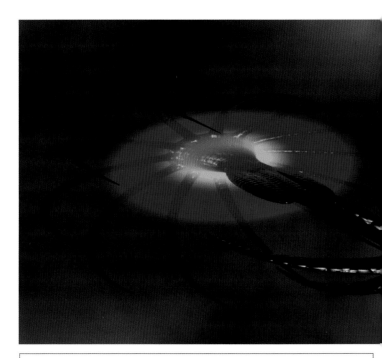

Future spaceships may allow us to travel at great speeds through space, but it is impossible to travel faster than light.

SCIENCE CONCEPTS

GREAT IDEAS

Einstein's theories – the Theory of Special Relativity *(1905) and the* Theory of General Relativity *(1916) – explain and predict the behaviour of all large objects in the universe. The phrase "large objects" means anything larger than a single molecule. Other rules (known as quantum laws) govern what happens inside individual atoms and molecules. Many of the things predicted by Einstein's theories were not discovered until after his death. He predicted, for example, that light could be "bent" by powerful sources of gravity. Astronomers did not discover these "gravitational lenses" until the 1980s.*

Some people claim to have been abducted by aliens. Greys like the alien on the right are seen in most abduction stories.

SPEEDING TO THE STARS

A more likely explanation is that the universe is simply too big, and the objects in it too far apart, for any contact with other intelligences to be practical. There is no point in making contact if visiting is going to be impossible. On Earth, we measure the speed of jet aircraft in Mach numbers, and the fastest jets travel at about Mach 5. A spaceship travelling at Mach 100 would take nearly 40,000 years to reach the nearest star. Allowing for accelerating from a standstill and slowing down at the other end, a round trip would take more than 100,000 years. Travelling at a faster speed would shorten the journey time. If we travelled at Mach 1,000,000, the round-trip would only take 10 years, but we would run into a very serious problem on the way.

FUNDAMENTAL BARRIER

The problem is that a speed of Mach 1,000,000 is faster than the speed of light. According to the theories of the mathematician Albert Einstein (1879-1955), it is impossible for anything to travel faster than light. He demonstrated mathematically that space, time, mass, and energy were governed by a set of very strict rules. Objects that increase their energy by travelling faster also increase their mass. At low speeds (below about Mach 1,000) the increase in mass is too small to have any affect. At faster speeds, an object's mass increases significantly, and the faster it travels the greater the increase in mass. According to Einstein's calculations, any object travelling at the speed of light would have too much mass to be able to move at all. Therefore, no object can possibly travel faster than light.

If scientists do find signs of life on Mars, it will be one of the greatest discoveries of all time. It will change the way we think about life on Earth, and about life elsewhere in the **universe**. But suppose it turns out that Mars has always been lifeless – it does not have to stay that way.

SHAPING THE SURFACE

If there is no Martian life to preserve and study, it will be possible to **terraform** Mars. Terraforming is the name given to the process of transforming the surface conditions on a planet so that it becomes more Earthlike. Mars is not only the most suitable planet in the **Solar System** to terraform – it is also the closest planet to Earth. Mars could be turned into a new Earth, providing new land where people can live and work. All that is needed for life to flourish on Mars is some water and a thicker **atmosphere**.

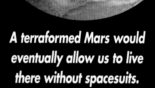

A terraformed Mars would eventually allow us to live there without spacesuits.

WATER AND AIR

Although there is no water on the surface of Mars, some scientists believe that the rocks just below the surface may contain large amounts of frozen water, especially around the planet's poles. If this water can be melted and brought to the surface, it will provide the basis for life on Mars. There might even be enough water to create lakes and seas. Some scientists have suggested that underground nuclear explosions could be used to melt the ice. A less violent alternative is to place huge mirrors in **orbit** around Mars. The mirrors would reflect sunlight onto the poles, raising temperatures and gradually melting the ice. If there is not enough readily accessible water on Mars, it is theoretically possible to import

water (in the form of ice) by collecting it from elsewhere in the Solar System and transporting it to Mars - perhaps from the rings of Saturn. Much of the water brought to the surface of Mars would evaporate — but that is part of the plan. Eventually there would be enough water vapour in the atmosphere for clouds to form and rain to fall. At the same time, solar-powered machines would break down some of the water into **hydrogen** and **oxygen**, and release these gases into the atmosphere. Provided there is enough water, we can give Mars a breathable atmosphere.

LIFE BY DESIGN

The 21st-century science of genetic modification provides terraformers with some exciting new possibilities. Some of the hardiest living things on Earth, such as **bacteria** and lichens, can tolerate conditions almost as hostile as the surface of Mars. With a little modification it would be fairly easy to produce bacteria that could survive on Mars. The bacteria could be further modified so that they performed an important function. For example, a type of bacteria that consumed iron oxide and gave off oxygen as a waste product, would be very useful on Mars. The surface is covered with rock stained red by iron oxide. Genetically modified bacteria would have plenty to eat, and would constantly be releasing oxygen into the Martian atmosphere.

Creating an atmosphere on Mars might take hundreds of years. In the meantime, explorers and colonists will have to rely on spacesuits when travelling across the Martian surface.

- *Mars is inside the Goldilocks Zone which means that there is potential for life to exist there.*
- *Mars is the closest planet to Earth and the most suitable for terraforming.*
- *There may be large quantities of water in the rocks beneath the Martian surface.*
- *Mars is known as the Red Planet because its surface is stained red by rust.*
- *Genetically modified bacteria could be used to produce oxygen on Mars.*
- *If there is frozen ice below Mars' surface, nuclear explosions might be used to release the water and create lakes and seas.*

If we were to terraform Mars, we would need to produce bacteria that could produce the oxygen we would need to survive on the planet.

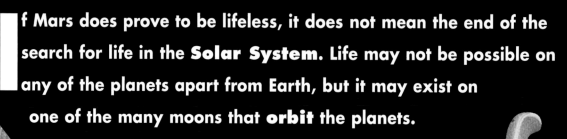

If Mars does prove to be lifeless, it does not mean the end of the search for life in the **Solar System**. Life may not be possible on any of the planets apart from Earth, but it may exist on one of the many moons that **orbit** the planets. The most likely candidate seems to be Europa, one of Jupiter's 16 moons.

TRAIL OF DISCOVERY

Four of the moons — Io, Europa, Ganymede, and Callisto — are large enough to be seen from Earth with an ordinary telescope. In the 1970s a Voyager spacecraft sent from Earth got the first good look at these moons and made many discoveries, including an active volcano on the surface of Io. Photographs of Europa showed it to be covered with a smooth layer of ice. Scientists had learned that the interior of Io was hot enough to produce volcanoes on the surface. Was it possible, they wondered, that the interior of Europa was warm enough for liquid water to exist deep beneath the icy surface. In the 1990s the Gallileo spacecraft obtained better photographs of Europa's surface. Some of the features shown in the new photographs suggested that there might be liquid water much closer to the surface than previously suspected. It is likely that Europa's ice is no more than 1,000 metres thick. Beneath this thin crust of ice, there is probably a vast ocean of liquid water.

A spectacular view of the craggy surface of Jupiter's moon, Europa.

WARMTH AND LIFE?

Europa is too far away to receive much heat from the **Sun**, so its ocean surface remains cold and frozen. Beneath the ice, however, things may be different. Scientists believe that Europa's ocean is kept warm by heat coming from the interior of the moon, which is probably made of molten rock. There are volcanoes on the surface of Io, and it is likely that there are undersea volcanoes on Europa. What makes this extremely exciting is the fact that scientists have discovered that undersea volcanoes can produce some of the strangest forms of life found on Earth. Deep beneath the Atlantic and Pacific oceans, undersea volcanoes known as "black smokers" provide chemical food for bacteria that need neither sunlight nor oxygen. Other strange creatures, such as tubeworms, feed on the **bacteria**. Life on Europa is therefore possible, and further exploration is already planned.

SUBMARINE THROUGH SPACE?

The first stage will be to send an *Explorer* spacecraft to orbit some 200 km above the moon's frozen surface. The Explorer will use a high-power **radar** system that can "see" through ice to map the extent of Europa's sub-surface seas. If the Explorer confirms the existence of large seas, the next stage will be to send a spacecraft to land a robot submarine on Europa. The submarine will melt its way through the ice and then sink down into the sea to search for signs of life.

This tubeworm can survive on bacteria that don't need sunlight or oxygen. Perhaps a food chain like this could exist on Europa?

CASE STUDY FACTFILE

- *Jupiter has 16 moons of which Europa is fourth largest.*
- *A layer of ice covers Europa, but there is probably liquid water underneath.*
- *The first active extraterrestrial volcano was discovered on Io (another of Jupiter's moons).*
- *Bacteria that need neither sunlight nor oxygen live around undersea volcanoes on Earth.*
- *A spacecraft will be sent in 2008 to circle Europa and find out the thickness of the crust using radars. A submarine would follow in 2030.*

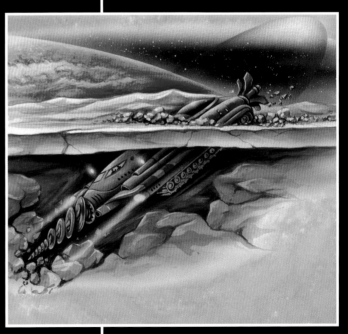

This artist's impression shows a robot submarine burrowing through Europa's thick ice in search of life.

Space is full of surprises, and nobody can tell when or where the next discovery will be made. By the end of the 20th century, most scientists were convinced that they had mapped and measured the whole of the Solar System. The recent discovery of other **"planets"** beyond the orbit of Pluto has forced them to redraw their maps of nearby space.

THE DISCOVERY OF PLUTO

The outermost planet, Pluto, was discovered in the early 20th century by patiently studying faint objects in the sky, night after night. If an object appeared fixed in place, it was a star; but if an object appeared to move slightly but steadily across the sky, it was a planet. When the discovery of Pluto was announced in 1930, some astronomers argued that it was not a true planet because it did not fit the pattern of the rest of the Solar

System — four small inner planets and four large outer planets. Pluto was small but outer, and it had a strange **orbit**. The other planets follow almost circular orbits and remain at a roughly constant distance from the **Sun**. In contrast, Pluto has an elliptical orbit shaped like a squashed circle; and it orbits at a different angle to the other planets. Despite its strangeness, Pluto was eventually accepted as the ninth planet in the Solar System.

STRETCHING THE SOLAR SYSTEM

With the advantage of more powerful telescopes, 21st-century astronomers have already made some startling discoveries. Using the same technique that was used to find Pluto, they have found other "planets" orbiting even further away. The largest and most distant of these new objects has been named Sedna. It was discovered in 2003. Sedna is about 1,600 km in diameter, and orbits the Sun at a distance of about 13 billion kilometers (about three times further away than Pluto). Sedna takes about 10,500 years to complete one orbit. Some scientists describe Sedna as a "planetoid", but others argue that if Pluto is a planet then Sedna is also a planet. Alternatively, instead of being the outermost planet, it may turn out that Pluto is the innermost example of an altogether different type of object.

The astronomer Clyde Tombaugh discovered Pluto in 1930.

THE OUTER LIMITS

The Sun, the planets, and their moons are the major objects in the Solar System, but scientists knew that there was more to the picture than that. Between the orbits or Mars and Jupiter there is a region known as the Asteroid Belt. This contains thousands of **asteroids** — lumps of rock and metal varying in size from the size of a bus to nearly 1,000 km in diameter. The largest of these asteroids are sometimes referred to as "minor planets". The outermost limit of the Solar System is marked by the edge of the Oort Cloud about half a light year from the Sun. The **Oort Cloud** is the name given to the region where most of Sun's comets are to be found. A comet is a dirty snowball made of ice and dust. **Comets** are smaller than most asteroids and have much less mass.

- *The planet Pluto was not discovered until 1930.*
- *Pluto does not follow the "rules for planets" that apply to the other eight planets in the Solar System.*
- *Sedna was discovered in 2003.*
- *It is almost as large as Pluto and orbits three times further from the Sun.*
- *The planet was named after an Inuit goddess.*
- *Most scientists do not accept that Sedna is a true planet.*

Inset: Pluto and its moon Charon.

Main: Artists impression of Sedna.

According to Albert Einstein, we may never travel to the **stars** because the distances are too great and we cannot travel faster than light. But scientists are constantly developing new ideas and theories. One day it may in fact be possible to build faster-than-light spaceships that can carry human passengers between the **galaxies**. In the meantime, there is at least one other possible method of travelling across the **universe**. However, travel by way of **black holes** and **wormholes** may be very dangerous indeed.

This illustration shows a black hole (orange) slowly pulling a giant star (blue) into its centre with its enormous gravitational pull.

BLACK HOLES

Black holes are the most powerful, dangerous, and fascinating objects in the universe. A black hole is created when a very large star explodes, and it is made of matter that is so tightly compressed it "disappears" from the universe. The gravity of a black hole is like nothing we have ever experienced — it is so strong that it sucks in light as well as any nearby matter. A black hole the size of a golf ball could absorb the whole of the planet Earth without measurably increasing in size. A black hole the size of Jupiter would contain more mass than a billion stars. A glowing disc, called an accretion disc, surrounds an active black hole that is sucking in matter. However, an inactive black hole (one that is not absorbing any matter) is just that - a black hole, invisible against the blackness of space.

WORMHOLES

An inactive black hole is invisible only in terms of light — if you could "see" with gravity, the picture would be very different. Black holes, even small ones, produce incredibly concentrated **gravity** that is much, much stronger than the gravity of stars and galaxies. Some scientists believe a black hole's gravity is strong enough to bore a hole through space to somewhere else. These holes are known as wormholes, although nobody yet knows for sure whether they exist or not.

If they do exist, then wormholes could provide the explorers of the future with a way of travelling around the universe. Wormholes may turn out to be short-cuts to the stars, or they could take us even further than that.

DESTINATION: UNKNOWN

If wormholes exist, we have no way of knowing where they will take us. A wormhole might, for example, lead to another part of our universe that is hundreds of **light years** from Earth. In that case, at least the explorers would eventually be able to work out where they were. But according to some theories, wormholes might be gateways to different universes, in which case the explorers would have no way of finding out where they were. Another theory is that a wormhole would lead to the same place in the same universe, but at a different time — so wormholes would operate like time machines. Whatever the destination, there is no guarantee that human passengers would survive a journey through a wormhole. The force of gravity might be strong enough to pull their bodies apart in a process known as "spaghettification".

This artwork shows a futuristic spacecraft leaving a wormhole near the planet Jupiter. These wormholes may allow rapid travel across our universe.

- *According to Einstein, space-time is warped and stretched by the force of gravity.*
- *Black holes have the strongest gravity of any objects in the universe.*
- *A black hole consists of matter that has collapsed in on itself and is millions of times denser than the superdense matter of a neutron star.*
- *Black holes may create wormholes in space-time through which it might be possible to travel across the universe.*
- *Wormholes might also enable us to travel through time.*

Films such as 'Back to the Future' explore the exciting possibility of time travel.

Air – the mixture of gases that makes up Earth's atmosphere. Air is about 78% nitrogen, 21% oxygen, with small amounts of hydrogen, carbon dioxide, and other gases.

Asteroid – a lump of rock in space ranging in size from 1-900 km in diameter.

Atmosphere – a layer of gas covering the surface of a planet or moon.

Bacteria – group of single-celled microbes that are among the simplest forms of known life.

Black hole – a object with immensely strong gravity – strong enough to "suck in" light – formed by the collapse of a supergiant star.

Carbon – one of the chemical elements that is an essential part of all "living" chemistry.

Carbon dioxide – a gas that is found in in the atmospheres of several planets.

Comet – a mass of ice and dust up to 50 km in diameter that orbits around the Sun.

Doppler technique – variations to light, radio, or sound waves that can be detected when an object is moving towards or away from an observer.

Electromagnetic spectrum – the range of wavelengths by which energy such as light, radio, and X-rays travel through space.

Extra-solar – describes any object orbiting a star other than the Sun.

Extraterrestrial – describes anything having an origin elsewhere than Earth.

Galaxy – a collection of billions of stars held in place by gravity.

Goldilocks zone – the region around a star where conditions are suitable for life to exist.

Gravity – a property of matter that produces an attracting force. Gravity is the strongest force in the universe.

Helium – a chemical element that is the second most abundant element in the universe. Most stars convert hydrogen into helium.

Hydrogen - a chemical element that is the simplest and most abundant element in the universe. Hydrogen is the basic fuel of stars; it also combines with oxygen to make water.

Interferometry – a technique that uses two telescopes to measure the position of an object very accurately.

Light-year – the distance travelled by light in one year – the basic unit for measuring the universe.

Milky Way – the galaxy of which our Solar System is just a very tiny part.

Moon – a natural object orbiting around a planet. The single moon orbiting Earth is known as "the Moon".

Neutron star – an object made of superdense matter produced by a supernova. Rapidly rotating neutron stars are known as pulsars.

Nuclear fusion – the process by which hydrogen is converted to helium producing vast amounts of energy.

Oort Cloud – The outermost reaches of the Solar System, made up of millions of comets orbiting at great distances around the Sun.

Orbit – the path through space made by an object that is "held" by the gravity of a more massive object.

Oxygen – a chemical element that is found in Earth's atmosphere as a gas. Oxygen is essential to nearly all forms of life on Earth.

Planet – a large object composed of rock or gas (in liquid or solid form) that orbits around a star.

Pulsar – a rapidly rotating neutron star that sends out two beams of high-power radio waves.

Radar – a technique that "bounces" radio signals off distant objects in order to determine information such as their size, shape, and distance.

SETI – the Search for Extraterrestial Intelligence, a project that listens to radio signals from space and analyzes them for signs of "artificiality".

Solar System – the Sun and the objects orbiting around it.

Space-time – Einstein's idea that space and time are just two ways of looking at the same thing, and that space-time is the basic fabric of the universe.

Star – a huge, spinning mass of gas that is tightly compressed by gravity.

Sun – a small and unusually bright star – the center of the Solar System.

Superdense – describes matter that has been compressed by gravity into a much smaller volume than is normal in the universe.

Supernova – a massive explosion caused by the collapse of a giant star.

Terraforming – theoretical techniques for altering surface conditions on a planet so that is resembles Earth.

Universe – everything that there is between you and the most distant galaxies.

Wavelength – the distance between the crests of the waves that are formed when energy travel through space.

Wormhole – a theoretical short-cut through the universe formed when a black hole bores through the fabric of space-time.

Copyright © ticktock Entertainment Ltd 2004

First published in Great Britain in 2004 by ticktock Media Ltd.,

Unit 2, Orchard Business Centre, North Farm Road, Tunbridge Wells, Kent, TN2 3XF

We would like to thank: Jenni Rainford for their help with this book.

ISBN 1 86007 592 4 HB   ISBN 1 86007 586 x PB

Printed in China

A CIP catalogue record for this book is available from the British Library.

Picture Credits

Alamy: 8b, 10tl. Corbis: 9r, 10-11c, 14tl-15 all, 24-25c, 26b. NASA: 5c, 6b, 6c, 7r, 8l, 11tr, 12c & br & l, 20tl, 24l.
Rex Features: 5r, 7cb, 21r, 29br. Science Photo Library: 2-3 & 18tl, 4-5c, 12cr, 13t, 16cl, 17 all, 18-19c, 19r, 22c, 23 all, 27 all, 28, 29t.